Many Creatures

A Song About Animal Classifications

by Laura Purdie Salas
illustrated by Sergio De Giorgi

Science Songs

Sing along to the tune of

 "Clementine."

Learn about the many kinds of animals on our planet.

PICTURE WINDOW BOOKS
a capstone imprint

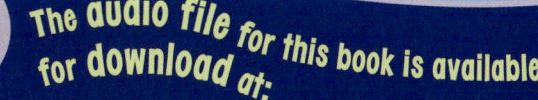

The audio file for this book is available for download at:
http://www.capstonekids.com/sciencesongs

Editor: Jill Kalz
Designers: Abbey Fitzgerald and Lori Bye
Art Director: Nathan Gassman
Production Specialist: Jane Klenk
The illustrations in this book were created digitally.

Picture Window Books
151 Good Counsel Drive, P.O. Box 669
Mankato, MN 56002-0669
877-845-8392
www.picturewindowbooks.com

Copyright © 2010 by Picture Window Books, a Capstone imprint
All rights reserved. No part of this book may be reproduced without written permission from the publisher. The publisher takes no responsibility for the use of any of the materials or methods described in this book, nor for the products thereof.

Printed in the United States of America in North Mankato, Minnesota.
092009
005618CGS10

 All books published by Picture Window Books are manufactured with paper containing at least 10 percent post-consumer waste.

Library of Congress Cataloging-in-Publication Data
Salas, Laura Purdie.
Many creatures : a song about animal classifications / by Laura Purdie Salas ; illustrated by Sergio De Giorgi.
p. cm. — (Science songs)
Includes index.
ISBN 978-1-4048-5763-6 (library binding)
1. Animals-Classification-Juvenile literature. I. De Giorgi, Sergio, ill. II. Title.
QL352.S25 2010
590.1'2-dc22   2009031942

Thanks to our advisers for their expertise, research, and advice:

Jerald Dosch, Ph.D., Visiting Assistant Professor of Biology
Macalester College

Terry Flaherty, Ph.D., Professor of English
Minnesota State University, Mankato

There are so many animals on Earth! They fly, swim, and waddle. They live in lakes, deserts, and grasslands. They have scales, feathers, and fur.

Scientists classify, or group, animals into different categories. Grouping animals makes studying them easier. The animals in each category have important things in common. Maybe they all live in the ocean. Or maybe they all have beaks.

This song introduces you to six animal categories. It takes place in the Everglades, a large swampy area in Florida. But animals from these six groups live all around the world.

We go paddling through the swamplands

Of the marshy Everglades,

Where the alligator watches,

And the great blue heron wades.

Many creatures fill our planet,

And we group them with these words:

They are reptiles and amphibians,

Mammals, insects, fish, and birds.

Alligators are cold-blooded.

They need sunshine every day.

They lay eggs, have skin of scales,

These big reptiles hunt for prey.

All reptiles are cold-blooded. Their body temperature changes with their surroundings. They must warm themselves with sunshine. Many reptiles eat other animals. Alligators, lizards, snakes, and turtles are examples of reptiles.

This amphibian's a tree frog.

It feels damp here in my hand.

Tree frogs hatch from eggs in water

But live most their life on land.

Like reptiles, amphibians are cold-blooded. Toads, frogs, and salamanders are amphibians. They have damp skin and usually live near water. They commonly lay eggs in water, and their young usually live in water. But adults almost always live on land.

Do you see that round-tailed muskrat
And her young one over there?
Mammals give birth to live babies,
And they have some fur or hair.

Mammals are warm-blooded. Their body temperature stays the same no matter how cold or hot their surroundings are. Mammals make milk for their young. Rabbits, panthers, and dolphins are examples of mammals.

In this swamp live many insects:

Beetles, ants, bees, dragonflies.

They have hard shells and three body parts,

And they see through compound eyes.

Insects are cold-blooded animals. They have hard shells called exoskeletons. Their eyes are compound. This means each eye is made up of a large number of tiny eyes.

We see largemouth bass and tarpon.

We see streaks of silver tails.

Fish have fins and live in water.

Most are covered with hard scales.

fish eggs

Fish are cold-blooded animals that have fins and live in water. Most of them lay eggs and are covered with scales.

Ducks and eagles, hawks and egrets—

All have feathers and strong wings.

They lay eggs and fly above us,

And they often cry or sing.

Most birds can fly, and all of them lay eggs. All birds have wings and beaks and are warm-blooded. Songbirds, such as mockingbirds, make musical tweets. Other birds, such as ducks or hawks, may quack or cry.

Many creatures fill our planet.

They might waddle, swim, or swoop.

Watch them closely; do some research;

Classify each in its group!

Many Creatures

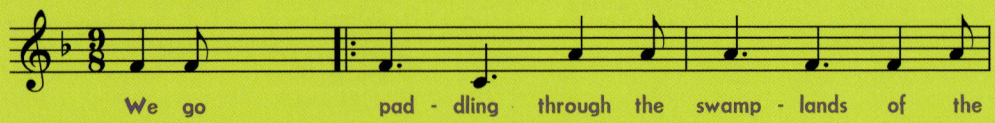
We go paddling through the swamplands of the

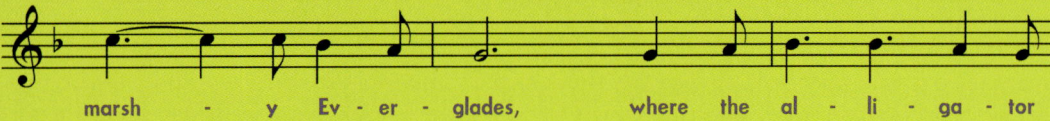
marshy Everglades, where the alligator

watches, and the great blue heron wades. Many

2. Many creatures fill our planet,
And we group them with these words:
They are reptiles and amphibians,
Mammals, insects, fish, and birds.

3. Alligators are cold-blooded.
They need sunshine every day.
They lay eggs, have skin of scales,
These big reptiles hunt for prey.

4. This amphibian's a tree frog.
It feels damp here in my hand.
Tree frogs hatch from eggs in water
But live most their life on land.

5. Do you see that round-tailed muskrat
And her young one over there?
Mammals give birth to live babies,
And they have some fur or hair.

6. In this swamp live many insects:
Beetles, ants, bees, dragonflies.
They have hard shells and three body parts,
And they see through compound eyes.

7. We see largemouth bass and tarpon.
We see streaks of silver tails.
Fish have fins and live in water.
Most are covered with hard scales.

8. Ducks and eagles, hawks and egrets—
All have feathers and strong wings.
They lay eggs and fly above us,
And they often cry or sing.

9. Many creatures fill our planet.
They might waddle, swim, or swoop.
Watch them closely; do some research;
Classify each in its group!

The audio file for this book is available for download at:
http://www.capstonekids.com/sciencesongs

Did You Know?

Many scientists believe the world's largest salamander is the Chinese giant salamander. It can grow to almost 6 feet (1.8 meters) long.

The whale shark is the largest fish in the world. It can grow to more than 40 feet (12.2 m) long.

Adult flamingos are pink. But their chicks are white or gray. The birds turn pink because they eat lots of pink brine shrimp.

Glossary

amphibians—animals that are cold-blooded and live part of their life in water and part on land

categories—groups

cold-blooded—having a body temperature that changes with the surroundings

insects—animals with an exoskeleton, three body parts, six legs, and sometimes wings

mammals—animals that give birth to live young, make milk, and have some fur or hair

prey—animals that are eaten by other animals

reptiles—animals that breathe air, are cold-blooded, have scales, and move on their belly or on short legs

scales—small hard plates that cover the skin of reptiles and most fish

warm-blooded—having a body temperature that stays about the same all the time

To Learn More

More Books to Read

Arlon, Penelope. *DK First Animal Encyclopedia.* New York: DK Pub., 2004.

Blackaby, Susan. *Who's in Your Class?* Columbus, Ohio: School Specialty Pub., 2007.

Kalman, Bobbie. *Is It the Same or Different?* New York: Crabtree, 2008.

Index

amphibians, 6, 10, 11, 22, 23
birds, 4, 6, 18, 19, 22, 23
cold-blooded, 8, 9, 11, 15, 17, 22
fish, 6, 16, 17, 22, 23
grouping, 3, 6, 20, 22
insects, 6, 14, 15, 22
mammals, 6, 12, 13, 22
reptiles, 4, 6, 8, 9, 22
warm-blooded, 13, 19

Internet Sites

FactHound offers a safe, fun way to find Internet sites related to this book. All of the sites on FactHound have been researched by our staff.

Here's all you do:

Visit www.facthound.com

FactHound will fetch the best sites for you!

Look for all of the books in the Science Songs series:

♪ Are You Living?
A Song About Living and Nonliving Things

♪ Eight Great Planets!
A Song About the Planets

♪ From Beginning to End:
A Song About Life Cycles

♪ Home on the Earth:
A Song About Earth's Layers

♪ I'm Exploring with My Senses:
A Song About the Five Senses

♪ Many Creatures:
A Song About Animal Classifications

♪ Move It! Work It!
A Song About Simple Machines

♪ There Goes the Water:
A Song About the Water Cycle